Want to know
a lot to do

Going to
the Theater

Florence Ducatteau & Chantal Peten

Clavis

NEW YORK

The school party is getting closer. Lisa and Arthur are working on a play with their classmates. Lisa will play Colombina, Harlequin's girlfriend. The director wants her to rehearse on a chair because during the show she will be standing on a balcony.

Meanwhile the dresser has her hands full with Arthur. Pantalone, the character he is playing, is supposed to have a big belly. Pantalone is an old grumbler who hates Harlequin.

The school play is about to start. The audience is ready, and the children who are acting have their costumes on. The crazy characters that you see were invented some five hundred years ago in Italy by the *commedia dell'arte*. The characters were funny and foolish. Before the show started, the actors would think of a short story. On stage they could improvise—invent on the spot—what they would do and say. Look, Harlequin is making funny faces again—of course! And Pantalone will probably get angry.

The theater in the old days

People have been acting since the time of the ancient **Greeks** and **Romans**. The performances took place in round **amphitheaters**. The players wore masks with mouths like megaphones so the spectators in the upper rows could hear them. The best plays of antiquity are still performed today. Those are tragedies (sad plays) and comedies (happy plays).

During the **Middle Ages** artists performed in town **squares** and in **castles**. Musicians, dancers, and acrobats made people laugh or dream by telling tales about battles, reciting love poems written by knights, or performing funny farces.

Actors traveled together and performed in different villages **along the way**. The leader of the troupe wrote the plays and performed along with everyone else. Everyone helped by making sets and costumes. The famous playwright Molière started as a traveling actor.

Later on many **theaters** were built so the actors wouldn't have to move around so much. The king and the rich spectators were allowed to sit on stage. All the other people in the audience had to stand. The stage was lit by candles.

Did you know
in the Middle Ages actors performed plays about Jesus in front of churches? They were called "mystery plays".

The theater now

Now we use the theaters in which plays are performed for other shows as well. Sometimes the stage and even the seats can be moved!

Most theater scripts are made up of **dialogue** (conversations between two or more people). A play is divided into **acts**. In between acts the sets (background decorations) sometimes change. Every act is divided into **scenes**.

The **director** is in charge. He picks the actors and decides how they are going to play and move on stage. The day before the **premiere** or opening night (that is the first performance of a play) there is a **dress rehearsal** with the right costumes, settings, makeup, and lighting.

The **theater manager** decides which plays are being performed in his theater, and he organizes tours. The theater season runs from September till June. In summer the actors play in festivals, like Avignon in France.

The illustration shows a rehearsal for Ubu Roi (or King Ubu), a play that the audience thought was scandalous when it was performed for the first time one hundred years ago.

Kinds of theater

If you like emotional plays, you should go to watch a **tragedy**. The characters are unlucky, and at the end of the play, someone usually dies....

If you love laughing, you should go see a **comedy**. A lot of funny things happen in comedies. The characters do stupid things, and people laugh with them. Some comedies aren't silly but show things that happen in real life in a funny way.

Did you know there are plays for all ages? There is theater for adults, young adults, children, and even for babies!

There are shows that aren't just plays. In a **musical**, actors sing and dance too. And in an **opera**, female and male singers sing to classical music.

Mime artists and **clowns** perform shows that have a lot of circus elements in them.

On sets and costumes

The **set designers** design the sets or décor. The décor is the background that shows where the actors are, for instance: in a room, on the street, or in a forest. Each part (or act) of a play is often set in a different place, so every act needs a different décor. The set designer first makes drawings and miniature models of the sets. That way the director can see if the sets match his vision of the play.

Afterwards the **set builder** and the **painter** make the real, full-size sets. Furniture and props (those are the objects that have to be on stage) need to be found or designed.

The **costume designer** sometimes buys costumes, but mostly he designs them himself. He makes drawings and looks for fabric and buttons to make the costumes. He works with the **makeup artist** (who does the makeup), the **hairdresser**, and the designer of the shoes, masks, hats, or wigs. The actors need several fittings to make sure the clothes fit right. The **dresser** helps the actors to get dressed and takes care of their costumes.

Did you know
girls and women weren't allowed to act in a play in the old days? The parts for women were played by boys or men!

Exercises for actors

Breathing exercises

Voice exercises and diction

Expression and grimaces in front of a carnival mirror

Did you know some actors are superstitious? Before every show they do things that they believe will bring them luck.

The journalists are invited by the producer. They will talk about the show on television, on the radio, or in the newspaper. That's how they advertise it. Of course the play is also promoted on the Internet or using social media.

Going to the theater is something special because every night the show will be different. Hopefully the actors will have a good show tonight!

In a minute three warning bells will sound to let the audience know to take their seats: DING... DING... DING! Then the curtain rises.

The **light technician** works the spotlights that light the stage and the actors. With light, shadow, and color, he creates the atmosphere the director wants. The **sound technician** takes care of the sound and the music.

Before the show starts, the actors prepare in their **dressing rooms**. They put on their costumes and have someone do their makeup. So they don't forget their lines, actors practice them a lot, first alone and then with their co-actors. They use emotions to show the audience how their character feels. When he is acting, the actor pays close attention to the other actors. He moves on the stage in a way that has been discussed and agreed upon. That way it looks best for the audience.

The **prompter** sits in a spot where the audience can't see him. He has a little book with the lines of the whole play. If an actor forgets his lines, the prompter whispers them to him.

When the play is finished, the actors take a bow. If the audience really liked the performance, they applaud for a very long time. Sometimes they even stand up or give the actors flowers. But sometimes they don't like the performance. Then they boo.

Puppet theater

There are all sorts of **puppet shows**. They are often—but not always—performed in a puppet theater. There are stick puppets, hand puppets, and finger puppets. Do you see them?

Puppet shows aren't always performed in a theater. Some shows take place in the street for a large audience.

Did you know
some Japanese marionettes are so big they need three people to move them?

Expressing feelings with your body

shy   cheerful   sad   in love   angry

Mock fights

Overcoming stage fright with relaxation and meditation

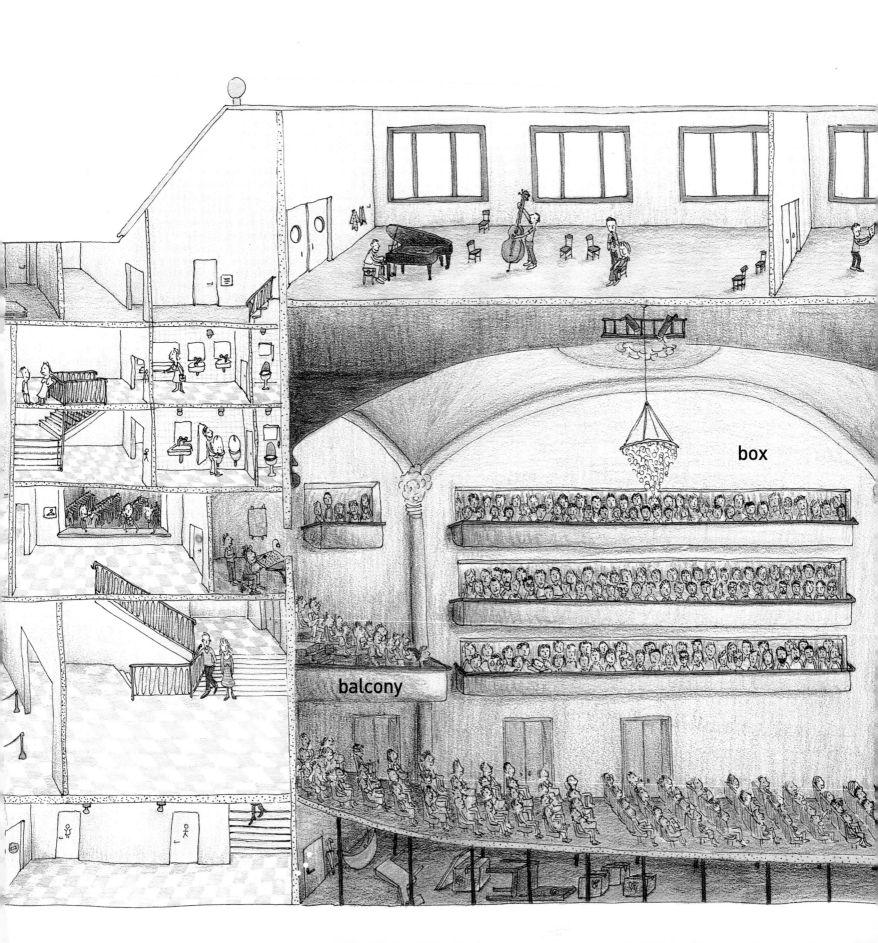

box

balcony

Inside the theater

This is a real theater with balconies. In front of the stage is the parterre. The chairs here are a bit lower than the stage. Some seats are higher. Those are in the boxes next to the **parterre** or in the **balcony**.

On the sides of the stage are the wings. You can't see the actors if they are in the wings. They wait in the wings until they are supposed to be back on stage. When the director wants the actors to move to their left on the stage, facing the audience, he tells them to move stage left, even though, as seen from the audience's perspective, the actors are moving to the right. That's also called house right. So stage left is the same thing as house right! And stage right is the same as house left! It's confusing—unless you work in the theater.

A lot of people work behind the scenes of a theater.

The **stage manager** is in charge of the technical functions of the theater: on stage, backstage, and in the catwalk – the space above the stage. His crew changes the sets between the acts and during the intermission, when the audience is relaxing. He makes sure the special effects, like the smoke machine, work. Or he opens the hatch through which characters can disappear.

The **stage technician** uses pulleys to lift the beams above the stage or to lower them. The beams hold the curtains, the sets, and the spotlights. In the old days strong men were needed to do this, but now electric motors do all the work.

To the theater

Lisa and Arthur are going to see *Romeo and Juliette* by Shakespeare. They bought tickets in advance and wait until the doors open. Their seat numbers appear on their tickets. An usher takes them to their seats.

It's the opening night. There are a few people in the audience who got tickets because they are friends with the actors or because they are journalists.

In a **shadow show**, the audience sits in the dark. A bright light casts the puppet's shadow onto a screen or a canvas so the people in the audience can see them.

There are puppets on strings too. They are called **marionettes**. The cross that connects the strings has to be strong. A marionette's movements can be smooth and look real.

In **object theater** all sorts of objects, like tools or vegetables, become characters who play a part!

Theater in the world

People all over the world enjoy theater. They all do it differently because every country has its own culture and history. Every type of acting has its own rules. Sometimes it is quite difficult to understand those rules.

In London you can visit the **Globe Theater**. Plays by William Shakespeare, the best-known English playwright, are performed there. Some of his best-known plays are *Romeo and Juliette*, *Hamlet*, and *Macbeth*.

In Japan you can go to watch **Kabuki** or **No**. In Asia the theater costumes are always very colorful.

In the African country Guinea you can listen to a **griot** or a **traditional storyteller**. He tells tales and plays music.

In Canada you can watch an **improvisation game**. The judge gives two teams a subject. They have a very short time to make up a conversation or an act about it. Afterwards the audience can choose which team they thought was funniest or best. And if the audience didn't like it at all, they can even throw a slipper to the stage!

Acting

Here is a section from *Cyrano de Bergerac*, a famous play by the French writer Edmond Rostand. It's been adapted so you can act it. Put on a long nose and your cape. Here we go!

Did you know
actors write the director's instructions next to the lines they have to learn?

look at a man in the audience

Hey! Tell me… why are you looking at my nose?

What is so special about it, or so weird?

Is it long and flabby, and does it hang

like the trunk of an elephant?

pretend you really have a trunk

Or is it crooked like an owl's beak?

Or do you see a zit on the tip?

look disappointed at the man in the audience

Or a fly that slowly walks on it?

pretend you are trying to watch that fly

Or do you, sir, maybe think it is a bit too large?

Large? Extremely large? Nothing more?

proudly, with a wave of your cape

pretend you cut it off with a pair of scissors

Use your imagination and be as brave as a musketeer;

then you'll change your tone:

(Aggressive:) "Sir, if I had a nose like that,

with regret

they'd have to shorten it on the battle field."

(Friendly:) "Dip it in your cup to drink;

it will be an excellent straw!"

(Describing:) "It's a rock! It's a heel! It's a cape!

Did I say cape…? No, a peninsula!"

in admiration

(Curious:) "When will this beautiful rocket rise?"

(Too friendly:) "Do you like birds so much you'll keep

a branch ready to let them rest?"

look at that man again

There, sir, you could have said all those things to me,

if only you had just a little more imagination.

Make your own hand puppet with moveable mouth

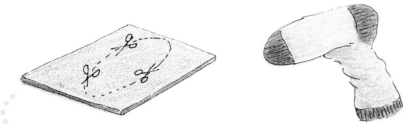

1. Take a sock from your mom or dad. Draw the outline of the bottom on a piece of cardboard that isn't too thick (a cereal box is about the right thickness), and cut out the shape.

2. Fold one end of cardboard about 1½ inches in from the edge.

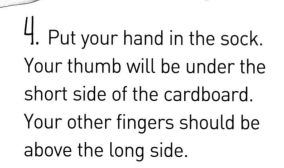

3. Put the cardboard in the sock with the short side against the heel. Place it so the bottom of the sock becomes the inside of the mouth.

4. Put your hand in the sock. Your thumb will be under the short side of the cardboard. Your other fingers should be above the long side.

5. There, your hand puppet is finished! Now you can decorate it as you like. Paste eyes – made of paper or buttons – on it. You can also use wool and colored fabric or cardboard to give it hair or a moustache, a tongue, teeth, a hat, arms…. You be the artist! When it's done you can be the actor and perform with your puppet!

Mini-quiz

1. What does the director do?

2. Do the sets in a play always stay the same?

3. What is the place called where the ancient Greeks gave theatrical performances?

4. What is dialogue?

5. What happens first, the premiere or the dress rehearsal?

6. What happens with the money you pay for a theater ticket?

7. What does the makeup artist do?

8. What is an actor with stage fright?

9. Do they call the most expensive seats in the theater "the gods"?

10. Why can't the audience see the prompter?

Answers

1. He is in charge of the show. He chooses the actors and decides how they will act.

2. No. They change to show the location of the actors. In one act a set could show a room; in the next act it could show a forest.

3. An amphitheater.

4. The words actors say to each other.

5. The dress rehearsal comes before the premiere. It's the last rehearsal before the play is performed for an audience. (The premiere is the very first performance.)

6. It is used to pay the actors and other theater employees.

7. He puts makeup on the actors' faces.

8. An actor who is very nervous or afraid before going on stage.

9. No, the cheapest seats on the highest balcony are called "the gods."

10. He is not part of the play. He whispers the lines if an actor can't remember what he has to say.

Find the seven differences

You've seen the illustration on the left elsewhere in the book. The illustration on the right looks different in seven spots. Find the seven differences.